Richard Seaford

Pompeii

Constable
London

Front cover: The Flagellation, a scene from the frieze of the Mysteries
Back cover: A Satyr and a Maenad

All frescoes, mosaics, bas-reliefs and sculptures are in the National Museum in Naples unless otherwise stated.

© 1978 Scala, Istituto Fotografico Editoriale, Florence
© text 1978 Richard Seaford
All photographs by Scala, except page 75 (courtesy of Fratelli Fabbri Editori) and page 63 (courtesy of Fratelli Alinari)

Printed and bound in Italy by
Cooperativa Lavoratori Officine Grafiche Firenze

Contents

Economy and Society

Pompeian society may seem to us familiar. The streets crowded with shops and taverns, the graffiti, the election posters and the dirty pictures, all this seems closer to a modern provincial town than to the distant grandeur of Roman civilisation. If we regard the sentiment *'lucrum gaudium'* ('profit is joy') as tastelessly blunt, that is because we recognise how apt it is to our own society. Pompeii allows a unique insight into the actual life of ordinary Italians of the first century after Christ, and so provides an invaluable addition to the picture of ancient society given by classical texts. But we should not be deceived by the superficial familiarity of the town into supposing that underneath the grand façade of classical culture ordinary life was, apart from some technological backwardness, much as it is today. Pompeian society was in fact at all levels very different from that of a modern town. Once we have understood this difference we will be better able to grasp the unfamiliar qualities of Pompeian art and religion and of Roman culture in general. For, like any other, Pompeian society is organic: we should not consider its religion, art, administration, material life and architecture as curiosities, entirely unrelated to each other. In most ancient communities the evidence for most or all of these activities is sparse. But Pompeii, preserved by the volcano that destroyed its inhabitants, can still be comprehended as a whole.

We begin with the activity on which all others depend, the production of material wealth. An obvious and fundamental difference from a modern town is the absence in Pompeii of any large factory. We see in its streets abundant industry, such as the making of bread and of clothing, but always in isolated units, never centralised in a factory. Production in Pompeii barely went beyond the scale of the household. Why is this? Why were, say, the numerous small fullers of the town never undercut, as they would be today, by the establishment of more efficient methods in a large fulling works? To put the same question in a different way: why was Roman civilisation, despite its towering cultural achievements and some impressive feats of engineering, so uninterested in efficient methods? Why was it so backward technologically? Particularly important are three factors, each of them effect to some extent as well as cause. Firstly there is the cost of transport in antiquity, which was great enough to prevent regional specialisation in anything save luxuries. For example, it would have cost so much to transport cloth from Rome that Pompeii had to make its own. And so Pompeii, being obliged to provide itself with all the necessities of life, could not specialise in a single basic product for national distribution in the way that Manchester for example came to dominate the English clothing industry in the nineteenth century. Apart from a few luxuries Pompeii was self-sufficient. The trade in luxuries is of course relatively unaffected by the high cost of transport. We know that there were gold-workers and jewellers in Pompeii. Her largest export was probably the excellent wine from the fertile slopes of Vesuvius. Another export as the famous Pompeian fish sauce. But it is interesting that even the fish sauce business, though largely in the hands of a single man (to judge from the frequency of Umbricius Scaurus' trade mark), was never brought under one roof, but remained apparently dispersed among the arrival points of the fishing boats.

The second factor is slavery. There are two brakes which slavery puts on the development of an economy. An unpaid and disinterested labour force provides no incentive to save labour by the invention and use of labour-saving devices, such as the spinning-wheel. Secondly, and more importantly, slaves were merely the property of their masters, 'speaking instruments' as they were known in law, politi-

General view of Pompeii with Vesuvius in the background.

cally, morally and legally distinct from the free man. And so, because manual labour and industry in general were activities associated with slavery, they were heavily tainted by the association. This is the ideological factor, probably the most important of the three. All material production, because characteristic of slavery, stood at the opposite pole to true freedom. And so the man who became rich did not in general become an active capitalist, he did not use his wealth to expand and modernise his business. He bought himself an estate, which was managed for him by bailiffs, and thereby freed himself of all association with servility and associated himself with the ancient landed nobility, the genuinely free. This ideology, so unfavourable to the development of industrial capitalism, is expressed in a famous passage of Cicero's *De Officiis*: 'The accepted view as to which trades and occupations are liberal and which are mean is as follows. To be condemned are occupations which incur ill will, such as money lending and the collection of harbour taxes. Illiberal and mean is wage-earning, where what is paid for is labour rather than art; for their wages are the mark of their slavery. We should

The bakery of Modestus, near the temple of Fortuna Augusta and the Baths.

Trade and Industry

The number of fulleries found at Pompeii indicate the high level of development of the wool industry in the city. In this painting one young man is brushing a cloth to raise the nap; another is carrying a wicker frame, which was used for bleaching or had a drying cloth spread over it. In his left hand he carries a fumigating bucket. The owl perched on the frame is sacred to Minerva, patron of all industries. So is his olive wreath.

Right   *Painting of a baker's shop.*

consider as mean those who buy from merchants in order to resell immediately; for they would make no profit without considerable dishonesty... All craftsmen, too, are engaged in mean activity, for there is nothing in a workshop appropriate to a free man. Of least merit are trades which cater for sensual pleasures: 'fishmongers, butchers, cooks, poulterers and fisherman' as Terence puts it... But occupations in which a higher degree of good sense is required or from which society derives no small benefit, like medicine, architecture or teaching, these are respectable for those whose status they befit. Commerce is, if on a small scale, to be considered mean. But if it is on a large scale, importing a great deal from various sources and distributing it widely and honestly, then it is not to be censured very greatly. Indeed, if such people become satiated, or rather I should say content, with their profits, and after many arrivals in port finally arrive on a landed estate, then we owe them the highest respect. But of all sources of wealth none is better or more attractive than agriculture, none more fitting for a free man.'

The operation of these factors is visible in Pompeii. In its relationship with the surrounding countryside it was quite different from a mediaeval or modern town. The cities and towns of classical antiquity have been called centres of consumption rather than of production. This means that they were convenient places for trading, governing and dwelling, within a predominantly agricultural economy. Neither the Roman state nor the Pompeian municipality gave assistance or encouragement to commerce and industry. The baron of mediaeval society owed his status, originally at least, to military supremacy over an area of land, which therefore required his presence. And the mediaeval town was allowed thereby to develop, by virtue of its developing manufacture, in opposition to the surrounding countryside. The Roman large landowner, on the other hand, would tend to regard the source of his wealth as a country retreat, leaving the running of the farm to the manager of his slaves so that he himself might pursue urbanity and politics in the town. The interests of Pompeii could not be set against the interests of the surrounding land, because Pompeii was itself governed largely by the free-born local landowners. The main harbour of the area was Puteoli, the modern Pozzuoli. Still, Pompeii's position near the mouth of the river Sarnus — since antiquity the land has encroached on the sea — allowed it to benefit to some extent from trade, notably the trade between Campania and the eastern Mediterranean. Transport in antiquity was always much cheaper by water than by land. But Pompeii never became essentially an *entrepôt*, like Ostia the port of Rome. It remained a community based on the surrounding land. Its characteristic manufactures, the conversion of rural produce into food and clothing, might almost as well have been performed on the farms. Its characteristic export, wine, was the surplus produced by the

*Frescoes of Cupids
performing manual
activities, in the triclinium
of the House of the Vettii.
The tasks illustrated here
are metalwork and
goldsmithery, work
in the vineyard
and winemaking.*

Vesuvius and Dionysos, the god of wine. Pompeii's largest export was probably the excellent wine produced in abundance on the fertile volcanic slopes of the mountain. To judge from the snake, which appears in all Lararium paintings, this was probably a propitiatory painting.

exceptionally fertile volcanic soil. How even the splendid town villa was but a development of the farmyard will be described in another chapter. For the time being it is enough to notice the rustic face of the town in such features as the agricultural instruments in the House of Menander, the oil presses discovered in the heart of the town, the table of standard measures prominent among the urban sophistication of the forum, the town guild of grape-gatherers, the seasonal agricultural fairs, and the recently discovered urban vineyards and market gardens.

True to its rustic origin Pompeian industry remained within the scale of the household and to some extent within the actual household itself. Thus cloth was generally spun and woven by the female slaves of a household to be treated in the workshops of fullers and dyers. Many of the workshops were also shops, with wide windows onto the street. In the painting in the House of the Vettii of the Cupids employed as metal-workers, one of them appears to be making a sale to a customer. The substantial house of Paquius Proculus

This very realistic mosaic of a variety of fish, most of them easily identifiable with the species still to be caught in the Bay of Naples, probably includes the ingredients of Umbricius Scaurus' famous fish sauce.

contained a bakery. But the five shops lining his house appear to have been independent of it. It seems that he may have disposed of his produce in the shop on the opposite corner. If so, then here perhaps is a delicate concern not to be associated too closely with commerce. The wealthy Roman, in devoting himself to higher pursuits, would leave the management of his household to an inferior member of it, usually a slave or a freed slave (a 'freedman'). Because the household was often the source of its owner's wealth, an agricultural business with its related manufactures, its servile administrator might often attain wealth and importance beyond the scope not only of his fellow slaves but even of the majority of the free-born. To take an exceptional case, the freedmen of the emperor's household might become fabulously wealthy and a power in the land. In Pompeii several seals have been found bearing the name of a slave along with his master's, as the administrator of his affairs; also the following epitaph: 'For a deserving freedman his patron erected this monument. In his life he spoke ill of no man. He did nothing against the will of his patron. There was always a great quantity of gold and silver in his charge. Of this he never desired to steal anything.' Furthermore, it might be in his master's interest to set up the slave in an independent business, the profits of which might eventually be used to buy his freedom. Of the farms and vineyards in the neighbourhood of Pompeii it has been calculated that as many as half may have been owned by freedmen. The phenomenon of the wealthy freedman was wonderfully satirised, a few years before the destruction of Pompeii, in the *Satyricon* of Petronius: Trimalchio is a Campanian freedman whose landed wealth and vulgarity are too vast to be credible, but who is entirely true to life in one important respect: he is unable, as a freedman to pursue civic office and political power, and so is irredeemably distinct from the ruling aristocracy whom he surpasses in wealth.

The Pompeian economy and society were, when compared with our own, both fragmented and static. It was fragmented firstly in that status cut across wealth. Equality of wealth would never knit a landed nobleman, a businessman and a landed freedman into a coherent group. Nor would poverty erase the free man's strong sense that he was very different from a slave. Neither rich nor poor formed a coherent class. Of similar tendency is the fragmentation into small units of production. Because the workers were not gathered into huge factories, as they were in the nineteenth century, they had no sense of a common identity or common interests as a class. The ancient world had no labour movement. Collective protest might take the form of a demand by a particular group for a certain right or privilege, even sometimes of a haphazard revolt by slaves, but almost never for demolition and reconstruction of the social order. Pompeii had its collegia, associations based often on a particular

Portrait of a man and his wife, usually supposed to be Paquius Proculus and his wife. The woman holds a wax tablet and the man a papyrus roll, which has led some scholars to suggest that he may be the advocate Terentius Neo.

Lucius Caecilius Felix, father of Lucius Caecilius Jucundus, whose business records have survived.

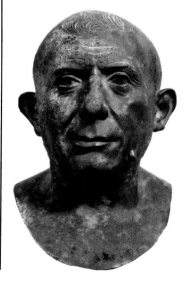

trade. They were frequently useful for mobilising support for a particular candidate for civic office. We read on Pompeian walls numerous election posters such as 'The united fruitmen with Helvius Vestalis urge you to make Holconius Priscus duumvir'. But, as we shall see in the next chapter, this does not mean that they were political organizations. Their primary functions were probably religious and social; and in this respect they are sharply distinct from the mediaeval guild, which generally exercised both regulatory control over its trade and considerable power, amounting sometimes to sovereignty, in the town. The fullers had a fine colonnaded building in the forum, provided apparently by their wealthy patroness Eumachia, in which to sell their wares. But there were no guildhalls.

As a result of all this, society was comparatively static. This fact is often obscured in Roman history books by the insecurity of national politics, the ever present danger of war and the rags-to-riches stories. Movement between classes is very different from movement of classes. A slave might acquire his freedom and even great wealth, and his free-born son might acquire the even greater status conferred by civic office. But the framework within which such social mobility occurred remained very much the same. Progress was made by the individual, not by society. Pompeii was never the scene of conscious class struggle. Even commercial enterprise remained at the level of the individual: the corporative enterprise was the exception, and generally unrecognised in law. The fragmented and the static quality of Pompeian society, which are of course two sides of the same coin, derive from an essentially agricultural economy, technological backwardness, slavery and household production. And at the same time they are reflected in the public life, art, architecture and religion of the town, as will emerge I hope from the following chapters.

Political and Public Life

In the war of 91-87 BC between Rome and her Italian allies, the Samnite town of Pompeii joined the Italians. After the war the inhabitants of Pompeii were conceded the citizenship of Rome, but had to accept, as a result of their resistance to Roman arms, a colony of Roman veteran soldiers and the name *Colonia Veneria Cornelia Pompeianorum*. From this time on the defenses of the town, although they survived until its destruction, became effectively unnecessary. After some initial conflict the Roman and the Samnite communities seem to have lived together amicably and, to judge by the racial mixture in the surviving magistrates' names, without continual domination of the one by the other. And public notices show that the old Oscan language was never entirely eliminated by Latin.

The governing body of the town and of its adjacent territory was the order of decurions (*ordo decurionum*), probably about one

hundred strong, composed largely of ex-magistrates, and correspond-ing roughly to the senate of republican Rome. The magistrates (two *aediles* and two *duoviri* [or *duumviri*] *iure dicundo*) were elected annually by the whole enfranchised male citizenry. The functions of the aediles were largely of an everyday administrative nature, such as maintenance of the public buildings and supervision of the market. The duoviri presided over meetings of the decurion council, carried out decrees of the council, and administered public funds. They also administered local justice, except for the more important cases, which were heard at Rome. Every five years were elected duoviri of parti-cular importance, the *duoviri quinquennales*, who performed the mu-nicipal census and had the important powers of nominating new decurions when the numbers had become deficient and of expelling unworthy ones. The magistrates were responsible to the *ordo*, except that the *quinquennales* appear to have had some contact with the central government at Rome. The town's official link with the capital city, and the defence of her interests there, were assigned to the *patroni coloniae*, who were nominated by the *ordo*.

This constitution implies the sovereignty of the people, who elected the magistrates and so indirectly created the *ordo*. But Pom-peii was no democracy. For one thing, women and slaves had no political rights; they were formally under the power of the head of the household, the *paterfamilias*. Members of the decurion order were required not only to be of free birth but also to possess a cer-tain amount of property; and certain of the meaner occupations were ineligible. But these requirements were not so much a cornerstone of the oligarchy as the legal sanction of a state of affairs that would have largely existed anyway. The basis of the Pompeian oligarchy was the economic fragmentation sketched in the previous chapter. The Pompeian poor, separated by variations of status and split into numerous small units of production, did not unite to elect a magis-trate committed to a programme of reform. In keeping with the household economy, political combinations tended to be vertical rather than horizontal. That is to say that vast inequalities of wealth and power, so far from causing the poor and the powerless to com-bine in political protest, made them dependent on wealthy and pow-erful individuals. Personal dependence was a feature of Roman po-litical life at all levels: for example, Pompeii chose influential men to represent it as *patroni coloniae* at Rome. A man would use his wealth and power to create a following, and his following to pursue a career of civic office (the *cursus honorum*) with its conco-mitant power and prestige. When we read a Pompeian election poster like the one quoted in the previous chapter we may imagine that the candidate bought the favours of the fruitmen in some way, or that he had some personal connection with individual fruitmen; but we should not suppose that he was the political representative

The Forum

The centre of public life was the forum, a busy rectangle surrounded by a colonnade on all sides. In the forum there were temples, municipal buildings and markets; there were no private houses. At the northern end (illustration below) is the arch in honour of Germanicus, between the temple of Jupiter, on the left, and the Macellum, the cereals market. Beyond it is another arch, in honour of Caligula.

of the fruitmen's economic interest any more than that the candidate supported by 'all the people of Isis' represented a political programme favourable to the goddess. Personal expenditure on public building and on public games might buy the favours of the entire town. The people thought that they needed the benefactions of the magistrates. And the magistrates, with their strong sense of civic prestige, needed the votes and the acclaim of the people. It was a fine thing to wear the special decurion dress on public occasions and to take your seat of honour among the *ordo* in the theatre and the amphitheatre. The purchase of prestige required considerable wealth. And so, because wealth was based on the land, the decurion order was composed largely of the wealthy landowners, with an apparent shift in favor of a more commercial class only in the last few years of the town's existence — a development assisted perhaps by an earthquake in 62 AD, which in destroying much of the town may have caused some members of the old ruling class to abandon it.

As a consequence of this political system, and in contrast with

The Basilica, at the southern end of the west side of the forum, was a kind of secondary forum, once roofed. At the far end is a raised tribunal, from which the magistrates dispensed justice. It is interesting that it was the Basilica, and not the temples, that provided the model for the later Christian churches.

our own, individuals were eager to exhibit their wealth and power to the people. This is apparent in the public life and even the public buildings of Pompeii. The centre of public life was the main forum, a long rectangle surrounded by a colonnade. Adjacent to the colonnade, facing inwards towards the centre of the forum, stood a row of statues of wealthy and powerful individuals, some probably of the Roman imperial family, others — the height of municipal honour — of local decurions. At the northern entrance to the forum stands a triumphal arch in honour of Germanicus, and a little way beyond it another, in honour of Caligula. The south side of the forum is taken up by municipal buildings: the decurions' council chamber and the magistrates' offices. At the southern end of the east side is the Comitium, where the people met to elect magistrates. At the southern end of the west side is the Basilica, a kind of roofed secondary forum, which was a centre for commercial transactions and for the dispensation of justice by the magistrates, who occupied a raised tribunal at the far end. There were no private houses in the forum. The remaining space is occupied by markets for cloth (the building of Eumachia) and for food (the Macellum, the cereals market) and by the temples of Apollo, of Jupiter, of the public Lares and of the emperor cult. These temples do not represent a power in the town separate from and potentially opposed to the order of decurions. The priesthoods were part of the *cursus honorum*; they were filled by the same people as the magistracies. The buildings surrounding a mediaeval Italian piazza may represent the competing interests of ecclesiastical, signorial or popular power. The forum, despite its historical connection and apparent similarity with the piazza, repre-

The temple of Apollo, on the west side of the forum, between the Macellum and the Basilica.

sents a very different pattern of individual honour within a static society.

The original forum of Pompeii was probably not the main forum but the 'triangular forum', a little to the southeast, built on a rocky and comparatively defensible spur. In the interior of this forum are the remains of a sixth century BC temple built in the Doric style. And beneath the spur, using its slopes as an auditorium, is the theatre. Temple and theatre are both symptoms of an important general distinction between Pompeii and Rome. Pompeii fell much earlier than Rome within the cultural area of the Greeks, who had settled on the Campanian coast at least as early as the eighth century BC. The ancient theatre derived from Greece. Although the Pompeian theatre was not built in stone until the early second century BC, the site had no doubt seen theatrical performances before then. The first stone theatre in Rome was built at least a century later. The Pompeian theatre is an Italian development of a Greek theatre. Greek drama originated in the dance and song of a religious chorus in a circular area, with the onlookers arranged on a hillside. And that is why, in the great period of Greek drama, the auditorium was still centered around a circular area (the orchestra), in which the chorus danced and sang their comments on the action, which took place on a small raised stage behind the orchestra. Later the action, which had originally emerged from the choral performance, continued to grow in importance, tending thereby to exclude the choral part altogether. And that is why at Pompeii the orchestra, though still in a sense the focus of the auditorium, has become merely semi-

This statue of a duumvir is most probably Marcus Holconius Rufus who, together with his brother Celer, had the theatre enlarged at his own expense.

Above left   The theatre, built in the early second century BC.

Above right   This bas-relief illustrates a scene from a comedy.

Below right   A mosaic found in the tablinium of the House of the Tragic Poet showing actors dressing up for the performance of a satyr-play.

circular and overshadowed by the architectural elaboration of the stage behind it. In mood the classical Athenian performances and the Pompeian were entirely distinct. Greek drama was a religious occasion, derived from popular ritual and performed in honour of the people's god Dionysos, whose priest had a seat of honour in the front row. Although popular rather than aristocratic, it was serious and sophisticated, based on the collective religious experience of the Athenian people. This combination of elements, giving rise to the unsurpassed phenomenon of Greek tragedy, was the product of Athenian democracy; it could never have occured in undemocratic Rome or undemocratic Pompeii. Drama at Pompeii, though possibly not without its religious trappings, was performed primarily to amuse the people, by virtue of which it increased the prestige of the magistrates who paid for the plays. For these benefactors seats of honour were reserved in boxes over the side entrances. The remaining seats of honour, in the front rows, were occupied by the decurions. The perfomances were probably mostly of farces, mimes and pantomimes. But, to judge from a few reproductions of theatrical scenes in the houses of the rich there were also tragedies, comedies and satyr-plays. Even the theatre building provided opportunities for individual purchase of prestige. Two inscriptions from the Augustan period announce that the duumviri Marcus Holconius Rufus and his brother Celer elaborated and enlarged the auditorium at their own expense. And the adjacent roofed theatre (the Odeon), similar to the main theatre but smaller and designed for music and recitations, was erected about 75 BC by the duumviri Quinctius Valgus and Marcus Porcius.

Behind the stage of the main theatre lies a colonnaded square (*quadriporticus*), originally a foyer for the theatre audience, but after the earthquake of 62 AD converted into a barracks for gladiators — ironically reminiscent, with its tiny cells on two floors around the quadriporticus, of a monastery. The gladiatorial shows were held in the amphitheatre at the east end of the town. This was constructed at about the same time as the roofed theatre, and by the same duumviri. The inscription survives in which they announce that for the honour of the colony they held *spectacula* at their own expense and gave the place to the members of the colony forever. This is the oldest surviving stone amphitheatre, and like the theatre it is more than a century older than the first construction of its kind in Rome. Gladiatorial combat, like the theatrical performances, derived from abroad and degenerated from its religious origin. Originating in combat at Etruscan funerals, a form of human sacrifice to the dead, it came to Campania probably as early as the sixth century BC, when Etruscan influence in the area was at its height. This religious conception persisted piecemeal into the Roman period: gladiators were sometimes known as *bustuarii* (funeral men), and

*The Odeon, the small
covered theatre,*
theatrum tectum, *built
in the early first century BC.*

*The outside of
the amphitheatre where
the gladiatorial combats
took place. These were
obviously the most popular
form of entertainment,
since the amphitheatre
held 20,000 spectators,
the theatre 5,000 and
the Odeon only about 1,500.*

The Amphitheatre

The games, ludi, *which took place in the amphitheatre consisted in combats between two gladiators, who fought to the death, although a good loser might occasionally be spared to provide further entertainment. There were also* spectacula *which involved gladiators fighting against wild beasts or wild beasts pitted against each other. The rivalry between the fans of different gladiators was very strong; in 59 AD it broke into a riot between the Pompeians and the Nucerians in which several people were killed (below).*

combats were sometime held to commemorate the dead. But the main purpose was to gratify the public's taste for excitement and cruelty. That gladiatorial combats were more popular than drama is evident from the buildings of Pompeii. The large theatre held about 5,000 spectators, the roofed theatre 1,500; but the amphitheatre held 20,000, which cannot be far short of the entire population of the town. After the earthquake of 62 AD the restoration of the amphitheatre seems to have occurred much more quickly than the restoration of the theatre; and the theatrical quadriporticus was turned into gladiatorial barracks. In about 165 BC the Roman dramatist Terence, who wrote Latin versions of Greek comedies, complained that a performance of one of his plays was ruined by a rumor that a gladiatorial show was about to begin. In 59 AD there was a riot in the amphitheatre between the Pompeians and the spectators from nearby Nuceria, reminiscent of violence between rival fans at a football match, but more serious in that several people were killed. According to Tacitus it started with some trivial incident: 'during an exchange of raillery, typical of country towns, they resorted to abuse, then to stones, and finally to steel'. The popularity of the gladiators themselves is apparent in inscriptions and graffiti found at Pompeii. Numerius Festius Ampliatus' advertisement for his troop as *totius orbis desiderium* ('the darlings of the whole world') probably contained an element of truth. For the shortness of the gladiators' life — every duel ended with the killing of the defeated, unless the audience out of respect for his courage expressed a desire for mercy — some small compensation was provided by the admiration they inspired, or were thought to inspire, in women. One Pompeian graffito calls the Thracian Celadus *suspirium et decus puellarum* ('the heart-throb and hero of girls'); another calls the *retiarius* Crescens *dominum et medicum puparum nocturnarum* ('the master and healer of girls at night'). It is perhaps a manifestation of the same phenomenon that a richly ornamented female body has been discovered under the lava in the gladiators' barracks.

The degradation of the amphitheatre was entirely unknown to the classical Greeks. How are we to explain it? In the same way, I believe, as we have explained the difference between Athenian and Pompeian drama; by reference not just to Roman psychology but to the kind of society by which that psychology was produced. Roman society was, we have said, essentially fragmented into different households, occupations and statuses. There is no Latin equivalent for our word 'society'. Of these divisions the most fundamental was between free man and slave, which was indeed so fundamental as to be absolute, thereby excluding any conception of a humanity common to them both. The slave was a 'speaking instrument', and gladiators were mostly slaves of foreign origin. Furthermore, and in sharp contrast to classical Athens, there is the political passivity of

A copy of the Greek sculptor Polycletus' spear-carrying Achilles, Doryphoros, obviously a portrayal of athletic beauty. This statue has steps leading up to it which indicate that it was probably the object of ceremonial crowning.

the people. Because they were mere recipients of benefactions from above, their own cultural traditions not only did not reach the level of Athenian drama, but degenerated into the trivial and the coarse. The system of dependence on wealthy individuals both caused the cultural vacuum and filled it. The epitaph of Aulius Clodius Flaccus records the hunts of bulls, boars and bears that he held in the Pompeian amphitheatre as duumvir. The tomb of Umbricius Scaurus, the manufacturer of fish sauce, is decorated with scenes of wild beasts and of gladiators. The provision of cruelty was a source of civic pride. The politics of the gladiatorial show are splendidly illustrated by some chat from Petronius' *Satyricon*; 'Good old Titus has a great imagination and a hot head. Maybe this, maybe that, but something will come of it. I know him very well, and he does nothing by halves. Cold steel he'll give us, no running away, and the butchery right in the middle where the whole amphitheatre can see it. He's got the money for it — he was left thirty million when his father died. Even if he spends four hundred thousand his estate won't feel it, and his name will live forever. He's already got some tough brutes, and a woman who fights from a chariot, and Glyco's steward, who was caught being enjoyed by Glyco's wife... I can almost smell the meal that Mammaea is going to give us, two denarii each for me and the family. If he does, he'll pinch all Norbanus' votes; he'll win the election easily. After all, what has Norbanus ever done for us? He put on some decrepit, half-baked gladiators who would have fallen over if you'd breathed on them... "Lay it on" roared the crowd; but they were nothing but runaway slaves. "Still" says Norbanus "I did give you a show".' The speaker is a vulgar rag merchant. But the attitude of the great and the good was, with some exceptions, little more attractive. Here is Cicero writing to his cultured friend Atticus; 'What a fine troop you have bought! I here that the gladiators are fighting splendidly. By hiring them out for a mere two shows you would have recovered everything that you paid for them'.

The remaining public buildings of note are the *palaestrae* and the baths. Here again, under the earlier influence of Greek culture, Pompeii was ahead of Rome. It was in the palaestra, a low building around a central courtyard, that the free youth of a Hellenistic town received a superior physical and literary training. It was regarded by more conservative Romans with suspicion, probably because, for their taste, it was insufficiently military. In some writers the palaestra appears as a place in which gymnastics consorted with reading and learned debate. In the second century BC a Samnite magistrate built for the youth of Pompeii a palaestra next to the theatre. Together palaestra and theatre formed the cultural centre of the town. In the Augustan period a much larger palaestra was built next to the amphitheatre. But although graffiti have been found of lines of

The Baths

Balnea vina Venus
corrumpunt corpora
nostra sed vitam faciunt
*(Baths, wine and sex ruin
our bodies, but they are
what life is made of).
Below, the Stabian Baths,
near the temple of Isis,
and, right, the hot room,
calidarium.
Roman public baths were
not devoted to health
and hygiene. They were
there for the undemanding
cultivation of leisure,
natural enough in a society
which had no trace
of admiration for work.*

Greek and Latin poetry, there is no reason to believe that Pompeii ever played a notable part in the intellectual life of its day (it is possibly significant that, in contrast to Herculaneum, no libraries have yet been found there). The spirit of the older palaestra seems embodied rather in an image found there of Greek athletic beauty, a copy of the Greek Polycletus' spear-carrying Achilles, which, to judge from the steps leading up to it, was subjected to ceremonial crowning. The gilded youth of Pompeii who frequented the palaestra were organized in their own quasi-religious association, the *Juventus*, of which membership was no doubt prestigious: it was sometimes mentioned by the young men when they came to announce to the citizens in election notices their worthiness to become magistrates.

Public baths were also derived from the Greeks, but were appropriated and developed with considerable extravagance by the Romans. Shortly after the arrival of the Roman colony in Pompeii and two generations before the first public baths in Rome, the old Stabian baths were modernised and new baths were built just north of the forum. The central baths were begun a few years before the final catastrophe and never completed. It is hardly necessary to say that all this building provided splendid opportunities for political beneficence by wealthy individuals.

Roman public baths were not devoted to health and hygiene. They were there for the undemanding cultivation of leisure, natural enough in a society which had no trace of admiration for work. Our nearest, but distant, equivalent is the café. *Balnea vina Venus*, runs an epitaph, *corrumpunt corpora nostra sed vitam faciunt* ('Baths, wine and sex ruin our bodies, but they are what life is made of'). And actually you might enjoy all three pleasures at once (including, after the growth of mixed bathing, heterosexuality). You went not for a quick dip but for an elaborate progress through the exercise yard (palaestra), undressing room (apodyterium), warm room (tepidarium), hot room (calidarium) and cold room (frigidarium). In Petronius' *Satyricon* our first glimpse of the wealthy freedman Trimalchio is in the exercise yard: 'We wandered around at first without getting undressed; or rather we went around having some fun, mixing with various groups at their games. Suddenly we saw a bald old man in a red tunic playing ball with some long-haired slave boys. It wasn't so much the boys that attracted our attention — though they were certainly worth looking at — as the paterfamilias himself, who was playing in his sandals with a green ball: when he dropped it he never bothered to pick it up, but a slave simply provided another from a sack... We went into the hot bath and then, baked in sweat, quickly on into the cold. There we found Trimalchio, with his body entirely covered with perfume, being rubbed down, not with ordinary linen but with cloths of the softest wool. Meanwhile, before his very eyes, three masseurs were drinking fine Falernian wine.'

The Villa and its Painting

As a consequence of its economic and political system, Pompeii gives a greater impression of splendid living than a modern town of comparable size does. Scattered thickly over the town among the one-room dwellings and workshops of the poor are the mansions where wealthy families lived with their slaves. Of these larger houses the nucleus is generally the atrium, an oblong area roofed except for a small central opening (the *compluvium*) and with bedrooms and living rooms ranged around it. Why were Pompeian houses built in this way, so unlike our own? The explanation is probably in their rustic origin. The farm is best protected against marauders and the climate by facing inwards, around a courtyard. But a town house is less exposed to these dangers. That town houses nevertheless continued to be built on this essentially rustic plan is partly a manifesta-

tion of the basically agricultural organization of society, as outlined earlier.

Nevertheless, an urban environment cannot fail to foster certain developments. The central yard, being no longer a farmyard, becomes roofed, except for a small central space to provide drainage and a water supply in a central basin (*impluvium*). The date and precise manner of this development are uncertain; but the result, at any rate, is the atrium. Secondly, the previous pressure on the surrounding rooms to face inwards is relieved, and then actually reversed by the insufficiency of the light now provided by the roofed atrium: the main living rooms, placed as they are opposite the street entrance, begin to face towards the garden at the back. The garden grows therefore in importance and is eventually, in the second century BC, embellished by the importation of the Greek peristyle, a courtyard surrounded by a colonnade. Hence the characteristically Italian phenomenon of the garden enclosed by a peristyle. The influence of the peristyle then spreads into the atrium, where it gives rise to a colonnade around the impluvium. Finally, two obviously urban developments are the building of shops (unconnected with the house) on either side of the street entrance, and the sometimes unhappy attempts to build a second storey onto the atrium.

A house of the older type is the House of the Surgeon of the fourth to third century BC. Entering from the street we pass through a vestibule into the atrium, which has living rooms and bedrooms around it and a simple shallow impluvium in the middle. On the side opposite the entrance, separated from the rest of the atrium by two wings (*alae*), is a group of three rooms of which the centre one (*tablinum*) was both the main living room and an open passage from the atrium to the back garden. The right hand ala leads into a lane. It has been suggested that the group of three rooms is derived from the farmyard's residential part, which was originally separated from the rest of the farmyard by entrances at the side, one of which has survived in the right hand ala.

In the House of Menander, on the south side of the Strada dell'Abbondanza, we enter a third-century BC atrium and pass through the tablinum into a second-century BC peristyle. Around the peristyle, on the model of the atrium, were added further living quarters, notably a large dining room (*triclinium*) and a set of baths. Behind the triclinium are sleeping quarters for slaves, an atrium containing agricultural equipment, and a stable-yard from which presumably the slaves went out every morning to work in the fields. It is interesting to see that here, in the secondary area to which the running of the farm is banished, the atrium retains its connection with agriculture.

The atrium plan might not have outlived its rustic function had it not also been suitable for town life. And in fact, as a result of the importance in political life of personal dependence on the great

The triclinium, the dining room, in the House of the Moralist (right): benches for reclining generally occupied three sides of the room. The peristyle, a colonnaded courtyard, of the House of the Gilded Cupids (far right). The atrium of the House of the Faun (below), looking through to the peristyle. The rain came through an opening in the atrium to fill the impluvium at the bottom, where the statue is.

household, the atrium functioned to some extent as the necessary public area of the house. 'Come out by the back door,' jokes Horace, inviting a friend to dinner, 'thereby avoiding the dependent who is waiting to see you in the atrium.' The Sicilian Diodorus, who died a generation or so before the destruction of Pompeii, called the peristyle 'a useful device for avoiding the confusion caused by crowds of people paying court.' A passage of Vitruvius, a contemporary of Diodorus, is worth quoting at length: 'Into the private rooms — bedrooms, dining rooms, bathrooms and so on — only invited guests have access. But there are areas into which anybody from the populace can come uninvited: vestibules, courtyards, peristyles and such like. Those who possess only average wealth do not need magnificent vestibules, atriums and reception rooms, because they pay their respects by visiting others and are not visited themselves... But men of high rank, who hold high office and have to resolve as magistrates their obligations to the citizens, must have princely vestibules, lofty atriums, huge peristyles, and groves and walks laid out to majestic effect.'

WALL PAINTING

Why is it that the activity of painting never received in antiquity the same intelligent esteem as it has in the Renaissance and the modern world? The answer is implicit in our first chapter. Painting, whether performed by slaves or free men, is a manual activity: and so, unlike poetry and rhetoric, it is not fit for a noble and truly free man. And in fact the painters of our period seem to have been of mean or servile origin. (A nice example is the painter Fabullus, who was so proud of his Roman citizenship that he painted the Domus Aurea in Rome wearing his toga — surely a sign of humble origin). As a result, we have almost no contemporary writing to assist us in understanding the significance of the paintings found at Pompeii. This difficulty is worsened by the fact that in general ancient painting has, unlike sculpture, perished. And so the paintings preserved by the eruption of Vesuvius represent a provincial fragment from a vanished tradition. The tradition was obviously largely Greek. How great was the Italian contribution? This is a point on which, given the absence of the crucial evidence, it is hardly surprising that scholars have disagreed. The following account is designed to avoid rather than to conceal difficulties of this kind.

A fundamental distinction between Pompeian wall painting and the wall painting of, say, mediaeval Italy is that the former is originally and persistently architectural in function. This point is best made by a brief description of the four chronological styles into which Campanian painting has been divided. The first style, corresponding roughly to the second century BC, consisted of the imitation in paint

An example of fourth style decoration, where figures were integrated into the elaborate architectural background.

of marble slabs, the vertical lines being accentuated by the insertion of pilasters. Horizontally the wall tends to fall into three sections: for example, in the atrium of the House of Sallust there is at the bottom a continuous yellow dado, then, above this, three rows of panels (the upper two with smaller panels), and thirdly, at the top, a frieze consisting of two moulded cornices enclosing a further row of painted panels. It has been suggested that this threefold division derives from the structure of an ancient type of house, in which the base was of large stone blocks, the walls of mud-brick, and the

35

The Styles

Left *Wall painting of the first style, in the House of Sallust. consisting largely of the imitation of marble slabs.*

Below far left *An example of the second style in the Villa of the Mysteries. Here the architectural function is developed, but now columns and pilasters frame illusory rather than real openings. The imitation of marble slabs persists particularly in the dado below.*

Below left *An example of the third style, in which the illusory opening was closed by rendering the architecture flat and merely ornamental.*

Below *The Room of Ixion in the House of the Vettii, a fourth style wall painting where the attempt to integrate the picture and the architecture was abandoned.*

Right *An architectural perspective, fourth style, in the south triclinium of the House of the Vettii.*

cornice of wood or stone. It is not difficult to see that once this pattern had established itself in the interior decoration of the house, it might persist even where, as in the entirely rubble walls of Pompeian houses, it had ceased to correspond to the actual structure.

The second style, which belonged roughly to the first sixty years of the Roman colony (80 BC to 20 BC), represents a radical development of the architectural function. The columns and pilasters tend now to be painted onto the walls. Previously they had generally stood framing doors and windows. Now they tend to frame illusory rather than real openings. The imitation of marble persists, particularly in the dado. And so does the threefold horizontal division, but in a complicated and sometimes barely recognisable form. Into the illusory openings are projected elaborate architectural vistas and often also (usually in the central portions) landscapes and figures. The surface is conceived — more so than in any other kind of painting — as a window onto what it represents. Even the figures of the famous frieze of the Mysteries, an unusual example of the second style, seem designed to be actually present in the room they surround.

The third style represents a modification of the architectural principle, perhaps through the influence of easel-painting or even of pictures woven in tapestries. Such pictures were small and complete in themselves, and therefore difficult to integrate into the architectural openings of the the second style. One solution of the problem was to close the illusory opening (at least in the central portion where the pictures were) by rendering the architecture flat and merely ornamental. This became the third style. Alternatively, the attempt to

Cupids as florists, part of the splendid fourth-style cycle in the House of the Vettii.

A Cupid riding a chariot drawn by dolphins, also in the House of the Vettii.

integrate the two elements was largely abandoned: the picture was simply surrounded by genuinely recessive architecture, as in the Ixion Room in the House of the Vettii. This is one form of the fourth style. Or the confines of the picture were broken asunder, and the figures took their place among the columns of the architectural vistas. The resulting impression is of a drama played against the elaborate Roman theatrical backdrop, by which in fact the style is undoubtedly influenced. This is the second form of the fourth style, and belongs to the last decade of the town's existence.

Painted architectural illusion turned the wealthy Pompeian's villa into a Hellenistic palace. No less indicative of his Hellenistic pretensions were the pictures themselves, the majority of which depicted scenes from Greek myth, painted in a style deriving from classical Greek art. Some indeed were copies of famous Greek paintings. Unlike post-Renaissance depictions of Greek myths, this style is not generally interested in nature: it is almost exclusively of figures, who often have the quality of statues. Pompeian figure painting, despite large and obvious differences, belongs to the same tradition as the sculpture of the Parthenon. One important difference is in their relationship to their original beholders. An archaic or classical temple frieze of, say, the victorious labours of Heracles, like the depiction of Christ's passion in a mediaeval church, represents events considered of importance to the well-being of the community or of mankind. For the Greek of the archaic and classical periods myths belonged to his living religion. They were celebrated in rituals at great festivals, one of which gave birth, in circumstances described earlier, to the theatre, where the myths began to be celebrated at an unparalleled level of artistic elaboration. As a result, classical Greek culture provided a series of myths so rich and powerful that, together with the Homeric epics, they continued to dominate the literary and artistic imagination of later societies, of whose living religion they now formed little or no part. The myths are now valued not for their religious and social significance but for the opportunities they provide for the gratification of refined sensibilities. This tendency, typical of the later or 'Hellenistic' period of Greek culture by which Pompeii was heavily influenced, has been named after its literary centre, Alexandria. And so what we see at Pompeii is a borrowed Alexandrianism, at two removes from the living myth.

The sculpture of the Parthenon shows the protective deities of democratic Athens and the great festival held in honor of her particular champion, Athena. And in an Athenian public portico was painted the city's greatest victory, against the invading Persians at Marathon in 490 BC. But the wealthy citizen of the static, fragmented society of Pompeii displayed in his pictures little interest in the past or present life of his own society. Devoted rather to the refined cultivation of his leisure, he must be looking ever upwards, towards the

Fourth-style scenographic decoration.

acknowledged refinement of Hellenistic culture. The pictures of everyday cultivated life are of Hellenistic customs. There is no point of contact between the decoration of the villas and the life of the adjacent streets. This generalisation is confirmed by the apparent exception. In the magnificently preserved House of the Vettii we find, apart from some mythological scenes, a number of depictions, in the large triclinium, of manual activities (weaving, metal-work, the vintage, farmacy), which unlike other such depictions are of a high artistic level. It is not impossible that these paintings, which belong to the fourth style, reflect the increasing commercial spirit of Pompeii after the earthquake of of 62 AD. But who is performing all this strenuous manual work? Cupids. Even where the artist is inspired by the bustle of the workshop, his conception is of mythological whimsy. These Cupids may equally well be depicted riding a chariot drawn by dolphins. Unadulterated pictures of popular life or local events are always depicted in a 'popular', inferior style.

If the myths selected to be depicted on Pompeian walls were no longer part of the living religion, what determined their selection? One factor is the theatre, in which the old myths had persisted in visible form. There may be cases in which this influence has operated unknown to us. In others, such as the pictures of Medea about to murder her children or of Iphigeneia confronting Orestes and Pylades, it is clear enough: for these are high moments of great tragedies. And in some pictures of the fourth style the figures are actually seen against a theatrical backdrop. There are also paintings and mosaics derived from the comic stage, which are among the

Iphigeneia in Tauris against an architectural background, from the House of Pinarius Cerealis. This painting was obviously inspired by the theatre.

most beautiful things found at Pompeii. It was only after embellishment by the theatre that low life ever appeared in art of high quality. Another factor is the influence of famous classical Greek paintings.

Further criteria for the selection of particular myths are harder to perceive. But it is important, for what it tells us about the Pompeians, that we should attempt to discover them. Let us take as an example Heracles. His labours are one of the most common subjects of archaic and classical Greek art. When we see them in archaic temple reliefs it is not difficult to perceive the spirit in which they were conceived, to perceive, for example, in the victories over the Nemean lion or the Erymanthian boar, a pride in the civilising struggle of harmonious physical prowess against nature, savagery and disorder. But Heracles' labours have not been found at Pompeii, pride of this kind being presumably quite alien to the owners of those elegant villas. He does, however, appear in Pompeii as an infant strangling the snakes sent by Hera to destroy him. For the early Greeks this was an awesome event: 'The serpents,' says Pindar, 'made their way through the open gates into the broad recess of the chamber, furious to wind around the child their swift-ravening jaws...' In the picture Heracles' parents are certainly alarmed; but we are more likely to feel amused. The spirit of the painting is closer to the Cupid driving the dolphins than it is to Pindar.

In another appearance at Pompeii Heracles has exchanged clothes with the Lydian Queen Omphale. Why did he do this? Cases of transvestism in myth usually derive from the ritual practice of which the myth is a projection: in this case the transvestism of Heracles was in origin probably a story to explain why it is that young men in an initiation ceremony dress as women (the original reason — that it is to strip them temporarily of their personality — being forgotten). Once the myth becomes detached from the ritual, it may take on a life of its own: it becomes material from which the poet and the artist may select and elaborate whatever pleases them. And this, in a nutshell, is the essential history of myth in the Graeco-Roman world. The transvestism of Heracles, its solemn ritual origin long forgotten, is for our painter a vehicle for erotic humour, as it is also for the (almost contemporary) poet Ovid: 'She gave him the dainty tunic dyed in Gaetulian purple. She gave him the soft girdle from her waist... She herself took the heavy club, the lion's skin and the arrows in their quiver. Dressed like this they feasted, and lay down to sleep side by side.' 'Oh shame,' complains Heracles' wife Deianeira, 'that the rough skin that you stripped from the flanks of the shaggy lion has covered a woman's soft body... You are victor over the beast, but she over you.' In the same way the tearing apart of Pentheus by the Maenads, derived originally from ancient ritual (the solemn dismemberment of the god embodied in the animal), and described in Euripides' tragedy the *Bacchae* as an event of solemn

Medea about to murder her children.

Orestes and Pylades in Tauris.

A comic scene.

42

The Myths

The Greek myths which are the subject of so much of Pompeian art were no longer part of the living religion, and therefore their depiction is often characterised by a lack of serious belief and a degradation into amusing, erotic or sadistic art which bears no resemblance to the solemn origin of the subject.

On this page Heracles strangling the snakes, in the House of the Vettii and Heracles and Omphale (detail) from the House of Marcus Lucretius.

Opposite Cupid and Psyche, from a house near the palaestra; the rending of Pentheus, in the House of the Vettii; the sacrifice of Iphigeneia (detail), from the House of the Tragic Poet; Dirce tied to the bull (detail), in the House of the Vettii.

and mysterious horror, in Pompeii seems to be conceived in the spirit of effete sadism.

In the wealth of the Greek myths, created though it was by the religious life of the community, there was detail enough to cater for the dramatic, humorous, sadistic and erotic tastes of a class devoted to leisure. And so the taste for sadism is expressed by the selection and conception both of famous events, such as the sacrifice of Iphigeneia and the rending of Pentheus, and of unimportant events in peripheral stories, such as the rending of Dirce by the bull. Erotic themes are numerous enough: Venus and Mars, for example, Dionysos and Ariadne, Cupid and Psyche, a Satyr and a Maenad. There is even an erotic painting from Homer's Iliad, a poem of small erotic content, of the scene in which Achilles is deprived of his slave girl Briseis on the instructions of Agamemnon. In Homer, the deprivation is a blow to the *honour* of Achilles, not to his heart: Briseis was given to him as a mark of his prowess in sacking her native city, and becomes an instrument in a battle of honour between the two proud warrior kings. But what interests the Pompeian artist is the last lingering moment before the cruel separation of besotted lovers.

The crudely pornographic possibilities of Greek myth were rejected by the wealthy Pompeian and his artists in favour of the more refined eroticism of suggestion. The story goes that the Centaurs, invited to the wedding of Peirithous and Hippodameia, became drunk and attempted to rape the bride. A picture of the attempted rape would have afforded a certain excitement. But the Pompeian artist painted the arrival of the Centaurs at the palace. One Centaur has placed his wedding gift, a basket of fruit, at the feet of Peirithous, and is kissing his hand. Behind Peirithous is an apparently nervous Hippodameia, and behind the Centaur more Centaurs massed on the threshold. For the cultivated spectator, who knew the story and so could not fail to think of its central event, the apparently innocent, courteous scene was delicately pervaded with imminent and brutish lust. The same impression is made by the picture of Pasiphae and Daedalus in the House of the Vettii. Poseidon, as a punishment

Left *Achilles gives up Briseis (detail), from the House of the Tragic Poet.*

Right *Peirithous receives the Centaur.*

for Minos' failure to sacrifice a handsome bull, caused his wife Pasiphae to fall in love with the bull; and the result of the union was the Minotaur. The delicately repulsive theme of the picture is the craftsman Daedalus showing to the queen a wooden cow in which she is to hide to entice the bull. On the adjacent wall is Ixion, whose sexual advances, less ignoble but no less illicit than Pasiphae's, were made at the goddess Hera. He has been brought by Hermes to Hera and strapped to a wheel, which Hephaestus is about to set in motion. Hera and Iris look on in an atmosphere of languid cruelty, while a woman seated on Hera's throne (Nephele?) seems to be requesting mercy for Ixion.

As a final example of the Pompeian conception of myth, take the story of Perseus slaying the dragon that was about to eat Andromeda. The moment in the story is so chosen and executed that we are unlikely to feel that Perseus, who is in the process of courteously unshackling the maiden, will be denied his sexual reward. 'Oh,' says Perseus to Andromeda in Ovid, 'those are not the chains you deserve to wear; better would be those that join keen lovers together.'

The figurative style of the classical tradition is born in myth, which has no interest in landscape. And classicism, the balanced composition of statuesque figures in a minimal environment, is the prevailing style of Pompeian painting. Opposed to it are three tendencies, which are not mutually exclusive. There is a tendency, particularly in paintings of the fourth style, to impart to the figures lightness and movement: in the Maenad, for example, in the House of the Vettii. There is an occasional 'impressionistic' tendency to dissolve the figures into their environment, as in the picture of the Trojan Horse. And there is a tendency to expand the environment, as in the painting of the punishment of Eros, of which the extreme form is landscape painting. The painting of mere landscape, or landscape with the insertion of a few buildings and figures, was probably (like pastoral literature) largely a product of the great cities of the Hellenistic era. It is urban society that inspires contemplation of nature. But given the fundamental difference between modern and ancient urban society, it is hardly surprising that Pompeian landscape painting is so different from the landscape painting of post-Renaissance Europe. The mediaeval growth of large towns in opposition to the countryside produced eventually in the civilised consciousness an absolute division between town and country that barely existed in antiquity. The civilised Roman town-dweller had a villa on his farm as well. The ancient pastoral poet could never have felt, in his sensual delight at the elegance of a rustic scene, Wordsworth's 'sense sublime of something far more deeply interfused.' And for the ancient painter, nature never assumed that life of its own that it has often had in post-Renaissance art: he did not set up his easel before an actual, inspiring prospect. The nature he painted

Venus and Mars.

Opposite *Ixion tied to the wheel (detail), in the House of the Vettii; Daedalus showing the wooden cow to Pasiphae, in the House of the Vettii; Perseus freeing Andromeda.*

48

Left   *The Maenad, in the House of the Vettii. This beautiful figure has an ivy crown, a thyrsos in her right hand and a tympanum in the left, and gold rings on her wrists and ankles.*

Right   *The Trojan Horse. We can see Cassandra on the left, next to the statue of Athena, rushing forward as the horse is drawn in. The impressionistic effect is meant to convey the idea of night and torchlight.*

was ordered: a garden, an orchard, a landscape centered around a shrine.

Nature did not have a life of its own: it was inhabited and controlled by the gods. So, too, was the house. The country gods (Silvanus, Bacchus, the Nymphs and so on) and the household gods (Lares and Penates) inhabited the two parts of a divinely ordered world. Within the confines of his villa the wealthy Pompeian might enclose both parts, not only by virtue of a shrine for the Lares in his atrium and a Bacchic sculpture or a shrine for the Nymphs in his garden-peristyle, but also through his wall-paintings of enchanted orchards or sacred landscapes: for they, like the painted architectural vistas, were probably intended to create an illusory opening in the wall. This represents the general Pompeian tendency to surround oneself with the sacred. We tend to regard a painting as nothing more than the representation of its object. But a number of Pompeian paintings may have been conceived as embodying the religious presence of their object, like a modern picture of the Virgin Mary. This applies obviously enough to the pictures described in the next chapter: to the Lararium in the House of the Vettii, on which the protective Lares and snake are painted together with the Genius of the paterfamilias, and to the protective deities painted outside the shop of Verecundus. And it is not entirely impossible that the portraits found at Pompeii have not wholly shaken off the function of the earliest Roman portraits, to embody the presence of the dead. And did the diet of Hellenistic sophistication also have an ingredient of personal salvation? The great frieze in the Villa of the Mysteries certainly seems to be conceived as imparting something of the great blessings imparted by the Dionysiac Mysteries themselves, which it represents

in such a way as to give the impression of their actual presence in the room. May the same also be true of the representations of the symbols of the Dionysiac Mysteries, such as the mosaic of a tragic mask and fruit? Are perhaps the Nilotic scenes intended to embody something of the power of the Mysteries of the Egyptian goddess Isis? That much of what we might consider merely decorative is in fact of mystical significance is a possibility important enough to raise here, but too complicated and controversial to discuss. A general perspective on the problem will, I hope, emerge from the discussion of the Dionysiac Mysteries in the next chapter.

Above *Detail of the frieze of Nilotic scenes.*

Right *Portrait of a girl with a wax tablet. The round frame was associated with the portraiture of the dead.*

Below *Mosaic of tragic mask and fruit.*

Religion

The civilised grandeur of Greek and Roman society is apt to conceal the fact of its relatively recent emergence, by a rapid process of economic development, from a tribal form of society no more developed than that of the North American Indians. The persistence of elements from its tribal past is fundamental to ancient culture, which is in this respect entirely unlike our own. The religion of the Roman republic has more in common with the primitive religions of Africa than with Christianity or Islam. Deity dwells neither outside the world nor within the human breast. At the festival of the *Robigalia* the Romans sacrificed a dog to Robigus, the spirit of mildew, in order to coax him into refraining from destroying the crops. The success of man's struggle with his environment requires the control of certain forces such as mildew, which are assumed by those ignorant of their real cause to possess a will of their own. The will of the numerous and various deities can be discovered by prophecy and divination, and influenced by the measures which we use to influence other people, such as gifts, commands and requests. The appropriate ceremonies are performed in the correct way to ensure the best possible relationship (the *Pax Deorum*) between society and the various unseen powers who might affect it for good or for evil, or to ascertain before undertaking some hazardous enterprise whether or not these powers are favourable to it. These, the essential features of Roman religion, can be found in primitive religion in general. But the development of Roman religion as a whole is unique, corresponding to the unique development of Roman society.

A characteristic feature of Roman religion, by which it is distinguished from the religion of ancient Greece for example, is the great importance of the household. In the Roman economy the well-being of each man, slave or free, depended on the fortunes of the household to which he belonged. And in the absence of an economic theory of society — something the Romans were of course very far from achieving — the varying fortunes of each household may appear to be in the control of unseen powers. The daily propitiation of these powers with offerings and prayer is a contribution to the prosperity of the house no less important than hard work and the careful keeping of accounts. The guardian spirits of the *penus*, the food store of the ancient Italian house, are the Penates, who together with Vesta, the deity of the hearth, represent the material prosperity of the household. Its temporal identity is represented by the Lares, the spirits of the ancestors, who in earlier times at least also represented its spatial identity, inasmuch as they were worshipped at the boundaries of the

The Lararium in the House of the Vettii. The central figure is the Genius, with the Lares on either side of him.

farm. The ability of the living paterfamilias to maintain the well-being of his home is in the hands of his own particular guardian or *Genius*. Painted on the Lararium of one of the Vettii at Pompeii is his Genius between two Lares. In sacral dress — his toga draped over his head — he is pouring with his right hand a libation and holding in his left a censer: he embodies the sacral duties of the paterfamilias. The Lares are pouring wine from one hand to another, an expression of abundance. The snake is probably a symbol of the renewal of the life of the ancestors in the living paterfamilias. For snakes are of phallic shape, and renew themselves by sloughing their skin.

The households of the expansive Italian countryside seem to have been isolated from each other to a degree impossible not only in nomadic societies but also for example in the narrow fertile strip of the Nile valley or the small isolated plains which constituted the Greek city states. Hence the importance in Roman religion of the household. But household religion cannot of course meet every need. The Lares resident at the boundaries of the farm were worshipped jointly by the owners of the adjacent properties at the country festival of the *Compitalia*. This practice, representing the overlap of public and private religion, persisted in the urban circumstances of Pompeii as the officially organised cult of the Lares Compitales, who lived no longer at rustic boundaries but in numerous street-shrines which have been discovered all over the town. And finally, as in the cult of the Vestal Virgins, whose duty it was to look after the sacred hearth of the Roman state, the household spirits are conceived of as protecting the Pompeian community as a whole in the cult of the Lares Publici, who had their temple in the forum.

The implied conception of the community as a single household is true in one respect: the religion of the Roman state, consisting in the accomodation of the unseen powers affecting society as a whole, was no less thoroughly practical than the household religion that it complemented. But we must not be deceived into thinking that the religion of the state required the general participation of its members. Such participation would hardly be favoured by the extreme fragmentation of Roman society into households and the consequently vertical lines of social organization described in the first chapter. The temples of Pompeii were no doubt used for private prayers and dedications, but their main function was to house the god together with the precious objects of his cult and the priestly performance of the correct rituals in his honour. They were not meant for a congregation, in sharp contrast of course to the later Christian churches, which were derived not from the temple but from the basilica. The Pompeian basilica was probably thronged every day with whoever cared to enter it. With some exceptions the tendency was for the knowledge and performance of the public rites to be concentrated in the hands of the appropriate officials. And so the state religion tended to become a weapon in the hands of the governing class. There was not even a distinction within this class between the secular and the religious power, because priesthoods were part of the magisterial *cursus honorum* and furthermore magistrates themselves had religious functions. Public religion came to be used for nakedly political ends. Writing about the extreme religiousness of the Romans, the Greek Polybius expressed the view that religion was originally designed for political purposes, its functions being to control the irrationality of the people.

A practical, polytheistic religion of this kind is doomed to nu-

The temple of Apollo, on the west side of the forum, with the bronze statue of Apollo.

merous failures: despite careful propitiation of the various unseen powers, battles will be lost, the crops will fail, the plague will not be averted, the state will tear itself to pieces in civil war. As a result, the religion is constantly in flux, ready both to accept new deities into its numerous, indeterminate pantheon and to modify its notion of those it already serves. Success in warfare inspired in the Romans a certain trust in the old religious ways which was easily outbalanced by the influence of the more impressive and the more anthropomorphic religions with which trade and success in warfare had brought them into contact. During the famine of 496 BC, for example, the triad of Greek agricultural deities, Demeter, Dionsyos and Kore, whose worship was popular in Greek southern Italy and Sicily, was brought into Rome and merged with the local agricultural spirits Ceres, Liber and Libera. During a plague it was only sensible to bring to Rome the Greek god of medicine Aesclepius from his famous shrine in Epidaurus. In the stress of the final stages of the struggle against Hannibal it was thought prudent to introduce the cult of the 'Great Mother' of Phrygia. It is, finally, little more than a manifestation of the same practicality that, after the Romans had conquered the Mediterranean basin and then torn their own society to pieces in savage civil wars, divine honours should be paid to the man who by victory had restored civil peace. 'We believed', wrote Horace, 'Zeus thundering in the sky to be king. But it is as an actually present deity that Augustus will now be honoured, once he has added to the empire Britain and great Persia.'

The gods of Pompeii fall into various groups according to their origin. First there are the gods of the old Oscan settlement, such as the agricultural Flora or the spirit of the local river Sarnus. Then there are the Greek gods: Apollo (one of the earliest inhabitants of the forum), Dionysos and his retinue of satyrs and maenads, who appear frequently in sculpture and wall painting, Zeus Meilichios, who was housed in the Strada di Stabia, Demeter, Athena and Heracles. The special guardian of the Roman colony, Venus, had her temple just south of the Porta Marina. In the forum, the temple of the 'Capitoline' triad Jupiter, Juno and Minerva, in imitation of the same deities on the Roman Capitol, expressed the older form of loyalty to Rome, to be superseded by the cult of the emperor represented by the temples of Fortuna Augusta and of Vespasian. The influence of the east appears largely in the cult of the Egyptian Isis.

The fragmentation of religion inherent in this international polytheism is in part an effect of the fragmentation of society. The manifold religious allegiance of each man was determined by his particular circumstances. A Pompeian baker, for example, will cultivate the Lares of his own house and, if his workshop is separate from his house, the Lares of his workshop, which will include Vesta, the patroness of bakers. If engaged in selling the bread rather than making it, he

Right *The Three Graces, the daughters of Zeus, personified beauty, grace and wisdom.*

Below *A copy of an original Greek statue of Apollo from the fifth century BC.*

will consider it prudent to cultivate the good will of Mercury. For Mercury is the patron of commerce: that is why he is represented carrying a bag of money on one side of the door of Verecundus' cloth-manufacturing shop together with, on the other side of the door, the colony's guardian, Venus Pompeiana (on a chariot drawn by elephants), Fortune (on a globe) and Abundance (holding a cornucopia and dish). Our baker might possibly also play some minor role in the running of a public cult. And he might furthermore consider it essential to his happiness in this life and the next to be initiated into the Mysteries of Isis or of Dionysos. When his wife had a baby, the deity to invoke was Juno Lucina. And so on. Cults which appear designed to embrace the whole of society, such as the cult of the emperor, had no *exclusive* claim on anybody. There was no organisation such as the Christian church to impose orthodoxy of belief and practice on the whole of society. And so there was neither heresy nor secularism. This does not mean, however, that there was no religious conflict.

In general the state was, for reasons already stated, not unfavourable to the introduction of foreign cults. The most notable exception was Christianity; but there were others, such as the cults of Isis and of Dionysos. In each of these cases the threat presented to the authorities was met at first by suppression of the cult and finally, after the failure of suppression, by its official adoption. What was the nature of the threat? In 186 BC the recently introduced Mysteries of Dionysos were brutally suppressed throughout Italy by the Roman authorities. The only surviving account of this episode,

by Livy, is the official version, and so hopelessly distorted. For example, we read in the same passage both that if you were initiated into the cult you were very likely to be murdered and that the cult was growing in popularity every day. But given the enthusiasm of the authorities for its suppression, we may well believe the allegation that the cult weakened loyalty to the state. Furthermore, from what we know of Dionysiac religion in general it is clear that the allegation of *conspiracy* reflected the reality that the adherents of the cult were initiated into sacred communities or *thiasoi*. Here then is the threat to the social order. The hierarchy of the Roman state was based on the organisation of society into relatively isolated households, each one ruled by its paterfamilias. The Dionysiac thiasos, on the other hand, represents a conception which, deriving from the more ancient organisation of society into tribe and clan, had retained a more vigorous life among the Greeks than among the Romans. In the unforgettable experience of mystic initiation, the Dionysiac thiasos united men and women of different households into a sacred community which ensured their happiness in this world and the next. And so its arrival in Roman Italy filled the vacuum left between the domestic and the official religions, providing that ecstatic solidarity characteristic of tribal ritual but long since departed from Roman religion. Such a movement, even though without secular objectives, must transcend the organisation of the Roman state. It was supressed in 186 BC but not eradicated; it continued to exist, though in forms less dangerous to the state. A quiet cult within the household would not arouse opposition. One such cult is represented by the famous frieze in the

Villa of the Mysteries. To this, which is incomparably the finest document of mystic religion in Pompeii, the rest of this chapter will be devoted.

The frieze depicts the ritual of initiation into the mysteries of Dionysos. For a full understanding of its meaning some preliminary general remarks are required about initiation, which is something that we find difficult to understand because our society has developed in such a way as to eliminate it. Among primitive societies initiation ritual is almost universal, and in particular those initiation ceremonies by which the young are made into full members of the adult community. The candidates in these ceremonies are subjected to certain characteristic experiences, such as beatings, purification, instruction, contests, special food, special dress, the revelation of sacred objects, death and rebirth, contact with the regenerative powers of nature, their first act of sexual union. The novices die as children and are reborn as adults; they learn the myths and ritual of the tribe; they experience the rites which they have from early childhood known as inevitable and yet utterly mysterious and terrifying; they pass from ignorance to knowledge, which may include sexual knowledge; they become full adult members of the tribe; they acquire, in effect, knowledge of the mysteries.

Among primitive societies this kind of initiation possesses a central position in the social and religious life of the community. And so, when such societies develop, its function cannot remain unchanged. It looses its centrality and social importance. But precisely because of this original centrality and importance, it does not disappear altogether, but persists as a vestige of the ancient order, with new functions derived from the old. Initiation into the Dionysiac mysteries is one such vestige. The tribal initiate dies as a child and is reborn as a member of his clan or of the whole adult community. Because this transition is more crucial than mere physical death, he is in a sense being initiated into the community not just of the living but of the living and the dead. The Dionysiac initiate is initiated into the thiasos, which is no longer the whole adult community nor even, like the clan, an effective part of it; with no effective reality in this world it tends to become a community more of the dead than of the living; initiation into the mysteries becomes a means to happiness in a shadowy association of the next world. The Dionysiac thiasos is the ancient clan in a new form.

The frieze is painted around the four walls of one of the villa's private rooms, interrupted by two doorways and a window. The figures, which are slightly smaller than life size, are painted over an architectural background (of the second style) in several scenes which, although in a sense distinct, are not wholly contained (as so often in Roman wall painting) in separate panels. In fact their continuity has been expressed by overlap between them in relationship to the

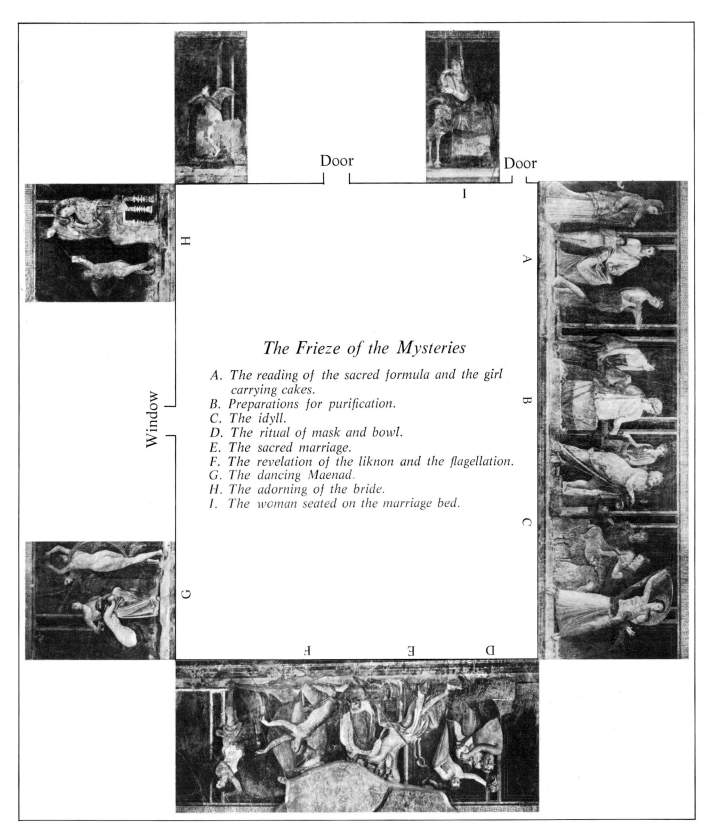

Door   Door

I

H

A

B

The Frieze of the Mysteries

A. The reading of the sacred formula and the girl carrying cakes.
B. Preparations for purification.
C. The idyll.
D. The ritual of mask and bowl.
E. The sacred marriage.
F. The revelation of the liknon and the flagellation.
G. The dancing Maenad.
H. The adorning of the bride.
I. The woman seated on the marriage bed.

Window

C

G

F   E   D

architectural background. Almost every detail of interpretation has been vigorously debated. The problem is of course that the object of our inquiry is itself a mystery. The secrets of the mysteries were known fully only to those who had been initiated into them. The following brief account is necessarily dogmatic, being intended merely to express what its author considers to be the essential religious significance of the painting.

The central group is the one immediately facing us as we enter by the larger of the two doors: the partly obliterated seated couple Dionysos and Ariadne, partners in the sacred marriage. In the adjacent scene to the right a crouching woman appears to be about to remove a veil from a basket. This basket is the sacred *liknon*, a winnowing-basket in the shape of a cradle, which was used to contain the sacred objects—usually a phallus and fruit—revealed to the initiates in the course of their initiation. The artist has painted here the moment just before revelation. But who is the initiate? It can be none other

The ritual of mask and bowl and the sacred marriage of Dionysos and Ariadne.

The revelation of the liknon and the flagellator.

than the kneeling, half-naked girl who is being flagellated (across the corner of the room) by the winged figure next to the *liknon*. Notice that the girl's eyes are shut. The word 'mystery' derives from a word referring to the closed eyes of the candidate for initiation. The revelation of the phallus probably derives from a feature of tribal initiation: sometimes the sacred objects revealed by the tribal elders to the novices are models of the genital organs, which may then be used to instruct the young in the secrets of sexuality. Flagellation also is a common feature of tribal initiation. But who is the winged flagellator? Numerous suggestions have been made. We would expect that here, as in general in Greek religion, the divinity is not a *determinant* but, at least in part, an *expression* of the ritual. And so the important clue to her identity is the function of the ritual. The function of flagellation, in tribal initiation and in its Graeco-Roman derivatives, is generally to be an ordeal and to impart fertility. A further clue to the flagellator's identity is provided by the defensive gesture that she is making with her left hand towards the *liknon*. Together with certain iconographical parallels, all this suggests that she is Agnoia, 'Ignorance'. As Ignorance she is simultaneously rejecting knowledge of the sacred objects, which are just about to be revealed, and torturing the initiate. The ignorance of the initiate, just before the final moment of revelation, her fear and trembling, are regarded as an ordeal. As in tribal initiation, the terror of the initiate is based on ignorance of what is to come. An ordeal, too, is the ritual flagellation of the initiate. The flagellation by Ignorance represents an assimilation of these initiatory ordeals to each other. The terrified ignorance of the initiate is conceived as a divine flagellation. Finally, when all is suddenly revealed, winged Ignorance is equally suddenly nowhere: she has taken flight.

The terror of the initiate seems also to be the subject of the scene which straddles the other corner of central and side wall, on the other side of the sacred marriage. A seated Silenos is holding up a cup over which a young satyr is leaning, while, behind the satyr, a young Pan is holding up a fierce Silenos-mask. Across the corner a girl seems to have just been startled by something in this scene; she moves away from it, while Silenos seems to be looking at her angrily. What is going on here? It is most unlikely that the satyr is about to drink from the cup. He seems rather to be looking intensely into it; and the context of the scene, as well as the holding up of the Silenos-mask and the terror of the girl, all this suggests that some *ritual* is being celebrated here, not an idyllic drinking scene. Perhaps it is a scene of catoptromancy (divination by images seen reflected in a shining surface) or of lecanomancy (divination by images seen in a liquid in a basin). If so, this would give a function to the Silenos-mask: it is being held up so as to be reflected in the bowl. The satyr-medium tells Silenos of the curious images that he sees there reflected, which Silenos interprets, as an oracle, to the girl; and it is by the contents of the oracle that the girl is terrified. The difficulty of this theory is to find a function for an oracle in a ritual of initiation, quite apart from the problem of why the girl should be startled by it. The Silenos-mask appears in other depictions of the Dionysiac mysteries, in which its only apparent ritual function is as a sacred object, to be revealed, like the phallus, to the initiate — a function which masks often possess in tribal initiation. If it has that function here too, then there is a thematic as well as a formal correspondence with the scene of revelation and flagellation on the other side of the sacred marriage. But if so, who is the initiate? Is it the young satyr, stimulated and confused, like the flagellated girl, by a partial revelation, the distorted reflection of the mask in the cup? St Paul may be using an image derived from mystic initiation in his first letter to the Corinthians: 'When I was a child I spoke as a child, I understood as a child, I thought as a child; but when I

The flagellation and the dancing Maenad.

became a man I put away childish things. For now we see through a mirror, obscurely; but then we shall see face to face.' However, the frieze as a whole seems to concern the various stages of *female* initiation. All the human figures in it are female, the only male figures being Dionysos and his mythical following (Silenos, satyrs and Pans). Is the startled girl a female initiate making an illicit instrusion on the mysteries of Dionysos' male followers and seeing the terrifying mask, which even the satyr-initiate has as yet seen only indirectly? The only certainty is that there has been no entirely satisfactory

interpretation of this scene. The mystery of why the girl is so startled is yet to be resolved.

The apparent correspondence between the two scenes of partial revelation, one on either side of the sacred marriage, is continued in the two adjacent scenes. Next to the flagellated girl there is a Maenad, one of Dionysos' mythical female followers, dancing and playing the cymbals (in front of a woman of unknown identity). Next to the startled girl there is an idyllic scene of a Pan playing the syrinx, a female Pan giving suck to a fawn, and Silenos playing the lyre. In both cases there is a sharp contrast between the terror of the initiate and the joy of the adjacent scene. What is the point of the contrast? Initiation is into the Dionysiac community, the thiasos, which may have no more than an other-worldly, mythical existence. Through initiation you might become a Maenad or a satyr, a member of Dionysos' mythical following, which is undisturbed by death. 'While we live in pain,' runs a Latin epitaph, 'you live renewed in the Elysian fields .... Maenads, followers of Dionysos, flock around

The girl terrified by the ritual of mask and bowl.

*The Silenos and
the Pan looking into the
bowl, with the fierce
Silenos-mask.*

the [newly-arrived] satyr in a flowery meadow.' But this blissful state is achieved only after passing through the terrors of initiation. Plutarch describes the state of mind of the initiates at Eleusis: 'The soul on the point of death has the same experience as the Eleusinian initiates... at first wanderings and wearisome hurryings to and fro, and unfinished journeys half seen as through a darkness; then before the consummation itself all the terrors, shuddering and trembling, sweat and wonder; after which they are confronted with a wonderful light, or received into pure regions and meadows, with singing and dancing and sanctities of holy voices and sacred revelations, wherein, made perfect at last, free and resolved, the initiate worships with crowned head in the company of the pure and undefiled...' This surely is the contrast expressed so beautifully in both the corresponding scenes of our frieze: the passage of the initiate from the terrified ignorance just before the consummation of the initiation to the idyllic certainty of the initiated thiasos.

So much for the central scenes. It now remains to discuss the

peripheral scenes on either side of them, starting with the scenes on the left, adjacent to the lyre-playing Silenos, which represent the preliminaries to the initiation. In his account of the Dionysiac mysteries in Italy, Livy mentioned three preliminary rituals: a meal, purification, and the making of prayers according to the *carmen sacrum* (sacred formula). All three are also typical features of tribal initiation. In the frieze the *carmen sacrum* is being read by a child standing in

The reading of the sacred formula and the girl carrying cakes.

Preparations for purification.

front of a seated priestess who holds a scroll. The meal appears to be represented by a girl walking away from the recitation of the *carmen sacrum* and carrying a plate of cakes. The purification is being prepared by the priestess seated with her back to us, who appears to have taken from the assistant on her left a twig which is being doused with purifying water by the assistant on her right. The water will then perhaps be sprinkled from the twig over the initiate. The

initiate herself may be represented by the mysterious figure entering to the left of the reading child.

Finally there are the peripheral scenes to the right of the flagellation scene, separated from it by a window and from each other by the larger of the two doorways. The first of them shows the adorning of a bride, with, across the corner, an admiring Eros. The second is of a contemplative woman seated on a marriage bed. These scenes, so far from being the mere decorative appendages that they were once thought to be, are vital to our understanding of the frieze as a whole. The fact is that the ritual of initiation and the ritual of ancient marriage have much in common. For example, the newly initiated man might be acclaimed thus: 'Hail bridegroom! Hail new

light!' This can only be explained by reference to tribal initiation, from which mystic initiation is derived. In tribal initiation the passage from childhood to adulthood is also the passage into marriage, or at least into the first act of sexual union. Hence the aptness of imparting fertility to the initiates by flagellation. As tribal initiation develops this practice declines: the sexual act, once general, comes to be performed by a representative pair, who are conceived as divine inasmuch as they embody the divine powers once conferred by initiation on the initiates as a whole. This is the origin of the sacred marriage of Dionysos and Ariadne depicted in the central scene of the frieze. Nevertheless, initiation and human marriage, because of their original identity, remain closely associated. Our frieze shows that a Pompeian female initiate might be conceived of as a bride, or even that she might be a bride. The room of the frieze might have witnessed both Dionysiac mystic ritual and wedding celebrations. If so, then the sacred marriage, which is derived from human marriage at initiation, is here in a sense reunited with it. By virtue of her marriage the bride is conceived of as entering through suffering into a divine and blessed state, in which she participates in the mysteries of sex embodied in the marriage of the divine couple.

The frieze falls into three parts: firstly the preliminaries (prayer, meal and purification); secondly the initiation itself, in which the initiate moves into the sphere of the divine; and thirdly the adorning of the bride and the assumption of the bridal bed. These three stages should be regarded as succeeding each other, but not in the manner of a comic strip: they do not appear to depict the successive experiences of the same initiate — in fact the figures who appear to be initiates are distinguished from each other by dress — but the successive *stages* of the transition from girlhood to matronhood. This tripartite arrangement of the frieze is probably derived from the ordering of the mysteries themselves. In the great mysteries of Demeter at Eleusis, of which we are better informed than any others, there appear to have been three stages of participation in the rituals: firstly the preliminaries, by which one became a candidate for initiation; secondly the initiation itself; and thirdly *epopteia*. The word *epopteia* means 'onlooking' and 'supervision'; the *epoptai* were the initiated, who looked on and supervised the initiation of others. To resume Plutarch's decription of the Eleusinian mysteries, those who have been through the terrors of initiation become at last 'perfect, free and absolved, worshipping with crowned head in the company of the undefiled, looking down on the impure uninitiated multitude of the living as they trample one another underfoot and are herded together in thick mire and mist.' Consider now the woman on the marriage bed. She is thought by some to be the initiate herself, by others to be her mother. Certainly she appears a little older than the initiates of the previous scenes. But to ask for her particular identity is perhaps beside the point, which is that she embodies the final *stage* in the transition from girlhood to matronhood. At the conclusion of the sequence she directs her calm and thoughtful gaze back across the room towards the flagellation, towards the ordeal of initiation that she has herself endured, and which she can now look back on in serenity.

The woman seated on the marriage bed, who here represents epopteia, *the 'onlooking' or 'supervision' by the initiated of the initiation of others. This woman embodies the final stage in the transition from girlhood to womanhood.*

Destruction

In August of 79 AD Pompeii and the smaller town of Herculaneum were entirely covered by an eruption of Mount Vesuvius. The following eye-witness account is taken from a letter written by the younger Pliny, about the death of his uncle the elder Pliny, to the historian Tacitus.

'My uncle was in Misenum in command of the fleet there. On 24 August, in the early afternoon, my mother drew his attention to a cloud of unusual size and appearance... He called for his shoes and climbed up to the best possible vantage point. It was uncertain from that distance from which mountain the cloud was rising (it was later known to be Vesuvius); it looked somewhat like a tree, more particularly a pine, rising as it were on a tall trunk and then splitting off into branches, perhaps because it had been carried up by the first blast and then left unsupported as the blast eased off, or perhaps even because it was borne down by its own weight and then spread out and gradually dispersed. It looked by turns white or blotched and dirty, according to the amount of soil and ashes in it. My uncle, as a man of learning and science, considered it important enough for a closer inspection. He ordered a boat to be made ready, and invited me to join him if I so wished. I replied that I would rather continue with my studies — it so happened that he himself had given me some writing to do. As he was leaving the house he was handed a message from Rectina, the wife of Tascus. She was terrified by the danger threatening her. Her house was at the very foot of the mountain, and so escape was impossible except by boat. From this dreadful situation she begged to be rescued. And so my uncle changed his plan. Learned curiosity was replaced by heroism. He had the warships launched, and went on board himself, with the intention of bringing help not only to Rectina but to the many others living on this lovely stretch of coast. He hurried on in the direction from which others were hurrying away, steering his course straight for the danger zone. So entirely fearless was he that he made a careful description of every motion and phase of the eruption precisely as he observed them. Ashes were by now falling on the ships, the hotter and thicker as they drew nearer to the shore, and then bits of pumice, and stones blackened, charred and split by the flames. Suddenly they found themselves in shallow water. The shore was blocked by debris from the mountain. For a moment he considered turning back, but when the helmsman advised him to do so he replied 'Fortune helps the brave. We must try to reach Pomponianus.' Pomponianus was at Stabiae,

Skeletons and skulls were frequently found in triclinia, dining rooms, where they were supposed to encourage one's appetite by the thought that life was not eternal and one should enjoy it while one could. In the Satyricon a slave brings in a silver skeleton during wine drinking and Trimalchio says:
'Eheu nos miseros, quam totus homuncio nil est! / Sic erimus cuncti, postquam nos auferet Orcus / Ergo vivamus, dum licet esse bene.'
(Alas, we miserable ones, for all men are nothing! Thus we will all be, once Death has carried us away. Therefore, let us live while we can still live well.)

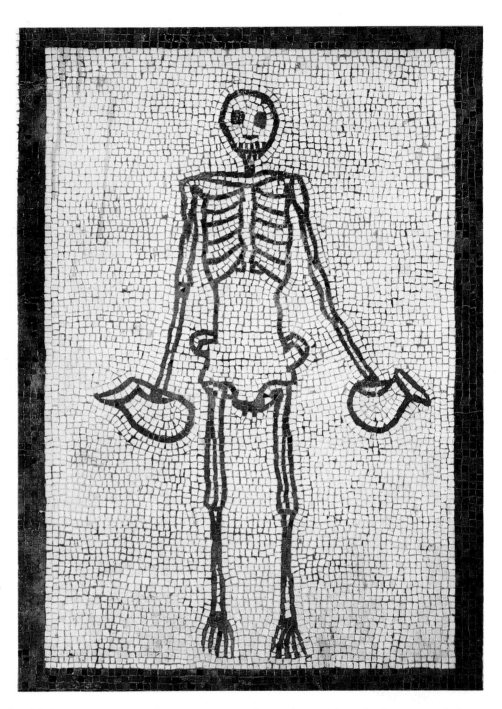

which was across the water on the other side of the curved bay. Him the danger had not yet reached. It was obvious though that it would reach him soon, and so he had already put his belongings aboard ship and was determined to escape when the contrary wind abated. This wind was favourable to my uncle, who landed, embraced and encouraged a terrified Pomponianus. In order to calm him by appearing composed himself, my uncle gave orders that he was to be carried to the bath. After his bath he lay down to dinner in good spirits — or at least appearing to be in good spirits, which demanded no less courage.

'Meanwhile on Vesuvius broad sheets of fire and tall flames were blazing at several points, their glare now emphasised by the darkness of night. My uncle repeatedly said, in order to calm the fears of the others, that they were peasants' fires abandoned in fear or deserted villas on fire. Then he went to bed, and actually slept — he was a stout man, and his consequently heavy breathing could be heard by those who passed outside his door. By now the courtyard outside his room was piled deep with ashes mixed with pumice-stones, so that had he stayed any longer in the bedroom he would never have emerged from it. He was wakened and joined Pomponianus and the others, who had not gone to bed. They debated whether they should stay indoors or make a break for it in the open. For the house was being shaken by huge and frequent tremors, and seemed to be swaying too and fro as if torn from its foundations. Outside, on the other hand, there was the danger of falling pumice-stones, even though these were light and porous. After weighing up the dangers they chose the latter. For my uncle it was a matter of choosing the more rational course, whereas for the others it was a choice of fears. On their heads they tied pillows with cloth, as protection against falling objects.

'Elsewhere it was by now daytime, but for them it was blacker and denser than night ever is. This darkness they relieved with torches and various kinds of lamps. They decided to go down to the shore to investigate at first hand the possibility of an escape by sea; but it was still wild and hostile. Then my uncle lay on a blanket on the ground and repeatedly asked for cold water to drink. Then flames and the smell of sulphur, which gave warning of the approach of fire, drove the others to flight and my uncle to stand up. He rose up leaning on two slaves, and then suddenly collapsed, presumably because his breathing was obstructed by the smoke, his windpipe being by nature weak and narrow and often inflamed.'

In another letter to Tacitus, Pliny describes the flight from Misenum: 'You could hear the shrieking of women, the crying of children and the shouting of men. Some were calling their parents, others their children, others their wives, or trying to recognise them by their voices. There were people bewailing their own fate or the fate of their relatives. Some in their fear of death prayed for death. Many prayed to the gods, but even more said that there were no gods left and that the world was now plunged in eternal darkness.'

Above *Three calques in the Pompeii Antiquarium.*

Right *A skull, reminder of death; a butterfly, symbol of the frailty and shortness of life; a wheel, symbol of necessity.*

Index